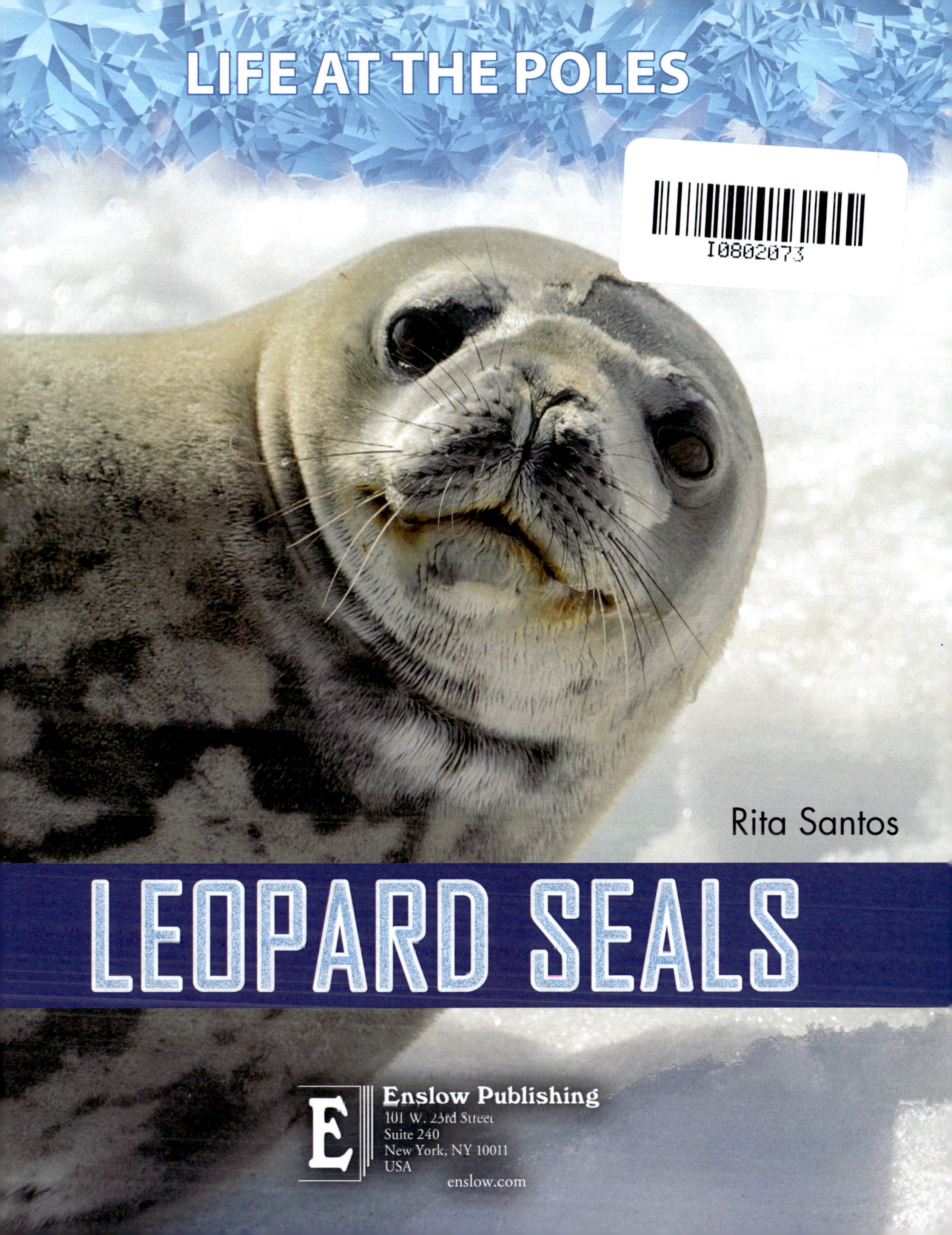

LIFE AT THE POLES

Rita Santos

LEOPARD SEALS

Enslow Publishing
101 W. 23rd Street
Suite 240
New York, NY 10011
USA
enslow.com

Words to Know

adapt To change in order to survive.

aggressive Dangerous or threatening.

blubber A type of fat that keeps some animals warm.

canine A sharp front tooth found in most meat-eating animals.

ecosystem A group of living and nonliving things and their environment.

endangered At risk of dying out.

predator An animal that hunts another animal.

prey An animal that is hunted by another animal.

social Living or spending time in groups.

solitary Alone.

species A group of animals that share the same traits.

wean The act of switching a baby's food from mother's milk to solid food.

Contents

1

ICE LOVING

Earth has two poles: north and south. The continent of Antarctica is at the South Pole. The area is very cold, dry, and windy. The temperature at the South Pole can reach -76 degrees Fahrenheit (-60 degrees Celsius). The leopard seal makes its home here. It is one of the most **aggressive** animals in the entire ocean.

LIFE ON THE ICE

The leopard seal spends most of its life in the frozen waters off the Antarctic coast. Some leopard seals have been spotted off the

The leopard seal is one of six types of seals that live in Antarctica.

Time for a Nap!
Leopard seals can sleep underwater.

coasts of Australia and South Africa. But it's not common for them to travel that far.

The ice that forms and floats along the coast is known as pack ice. The little time these seals spend out of the water is spent on this ice. Its body has **adapted** to survive in this harsh environment.

TRUE SEALS

Leopard seals are the second largest **species** of seal. Only the elephant seal is larger. Leopard seals can grow from 7.9 to 11.5 feet (2.4 to 3.5 m) long. They may weigh

The leopard seal's layer of **blubber** allows it to stay warm in the Antarctic.

between 440 and 1,320 pounds (about 200 to 600 kg).

The leopard seal's name comes from its coat. It is dark gray or silver with "leopard" spots. A thick layer of blubber helps keep it warm. Leopard seals are "true seals." This means they have no ear flaps. Above the water they can hear about as well as people. Underwater, they can hear much better. They have short, clear whiskers that help them track their **prey**.

The leopard seal has adapted to stay warm in the cold. It is also a dangerous **predator**.

2

KILLER SMILE

The leopard seal has a longer body than most other seals. It is also stronger than other seals. Its large front flippers help it to move quickly through the water. It has a very large head. Its sharp **canine** teeth make it a

The leopard seal's mouth curls up in a "smile," but that does not mean the animal is friendly.

Open wide! The leopard seal has sharp teeth that it uses to chew up its prey.

fierce hunter. The shape of its mouth can makes it look like it is smiling.

AGGRESSIVE REPUTATION

Leopard seals are known to be aggressive. They will attack prey that is larger than

Dinner Time

Like humans, leopard seals prefer certain tastes. They will move to an area based on what they like to eat.

they are! These seals may eat fish, sea birds, squid, penguins, shellfish, and even other seals.

Leopard seals can and do eat almost anything they can find. But a big part of their diet is krill. These are small, shrimp-like creatures. The seals' back teeth have a special shape. This allows them to strain the krill from the water as they swim.

HOW THEY HUNT

One of the leopard seal's favorite meals is penguin. The seals are one of the only

A leopard seal goes after a penguin in Antarctica.

animals that hunt adult emperor penguins. The seals will float close to the edge of ice floats where penguins are resting. When the birds jump into the water to hunt their own food, the seal's hunt begins. They can reach speeds of 25 miles (40 km) an hour.

The leopard seal's only natural predator is the killer whale. Leopard seals are **solitary** hunters. Killer whales hunt in packs. One of their common hunting methods is to trap a seal on a piece of ice. Then the whales work together to form a wave. This will knock the seal into the water and their waiting jaws.

3

SEAL FAMILIES

Leopard seals are not very **social**. They prefer to live alone. It's rare to see adult leopard seals together unless it is mating season.

CHOOSING MATES

Leopard seals spend most of their time in the cold waters of Antarctica. This makes it hard

Seal Sounds

Male leopard seals have five different types of calls.

for scientists to study them. They are not sure how leopard seals choose their mates. Scientists have noticed that adult seals make more noise during November and January. This is the time when seals are choosing their mates. Scientists believe the loud seal calls may help them find their partners.

A leopard seal mother and her pup rest on the ice.

Most seals mate on land. Leopard seals stay in the water to mate. Males will often mate with more than one female during the breeding season. But once February comes, the males go back to living alone. Nine months later, during the Antarctic summer, female seals will give birth to pups.

ICE DENS

To prepare for her new pup, a female seal digs a hole in the pack ice. It can take her months to finish the den. Most leopard seals have one pup per season. When it's born, the pup weighs about 66 pounds (30 kg). The mother and pup will stay in their den for about a month until the pup is ready to **wean**.

Adult leopard seals can dive underwater for 15 to 30 minutes. Young seals can only

A leopard seal pup will double in size in the first three months of its life.

dive for about seven minutes. During the winter, krill are too deep in the ocean for young seals to reach. The young seals may work together to learn how to hunt larger prey, like penguins.

4

CHANGING PLANET

Many polar animals are on the **endangered** species list. The leopard seal is not on the list. This does not mean that this seal will always be safe. Climate change is having a huge effect on Antarctica. How will leopard seals adapt to a changing world?

ADAPTING TO CLIMATE CHANGE

Climate change is causing the temperature of Earth to rise. This means that oceans also get warmer. The pack ice shrinks. Leopard seals need the ice to hunt and have pups. Leopard seals are one of several seal species

A leopard seal swims under the ice as it waits for prey to jump in the water.

that need ice to survive. Their thick layers of blubber help them stay warm in freezing waters. This could make adapting to life in warmer climates difficult. Scientists are not sure if leopard seals could survive the loss of their habitat. There is a lot we can still learn about the leopard seal if we protect the environment.

Like many animals who live at the poles, the leopard seal may soon feel the effects of global climate change.

Unwelcome Visitors

Scientists in Antarctica study leopard seals from small boats. Leopard seals have been known to attack these boats.

PROTECTING LEOPARD SEALS

Leopard seals may not be endangered, but most of of their food supply is. Many of the leopard seal's favorite meals, like penguins, need krill to survive. The krill eat the algae that blooms on sea ice. As the ice melts, there's less food for the krill. This means there is less food for the other animals. People can help protect leopard seals by ensuring the safety of their food supply.

ACTIVITY

ROLES AT THE POLES

Everything in an **ecosystem** is connected. A food web shows all the ways plants and animals in an ecosystem connect to each other. A simple food web might look like this:

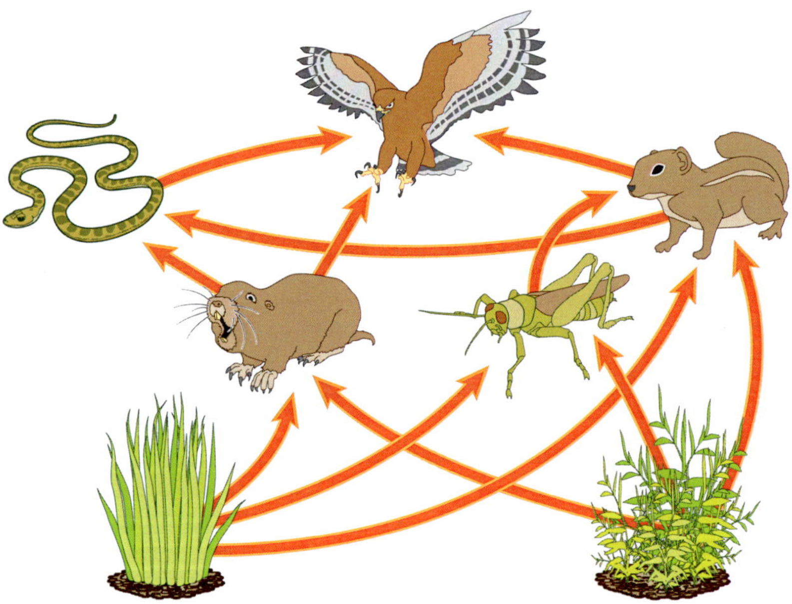

Living things gain energy when they eat. In a food web, arrows point in the direction the energy flows. The grasshopper gets energy from plants and the hawk gets energy from eating the snake.

You have just learned about the leopard seal and how it lives in Antarctica. What else lives there? Read over the list of animals found at the Poles.

ANIMALS AND MARINE LIFE OF ANTARCTICA

- Emperor penguins
- Killer whales (Orcas)
- Leopard seals
- Antarctic silverfish
- Krill
- Squid
- Sea birds

Think about what those animals eat. What does a leopard seal eat? What eats the leopard seal? You may need to do some research. Finally, make a food web (like the example shown). Show as many connections as you can.

Learn More

BOOKS

Beltran, Roxanne, and Patrick Robinson. *A Seal Named Patches*. Anchorage, AK: University of Alaska, 2017.

Gifford, Clive. *Polar Lands*. New York, NY: Kingfisher, 2017.

Snyder, Eleanor. *Alarming Leopard Seals*. New York, NY: Gareth Stevens, 2016.

WEBSITES

National Geographic Crittercam Leopard Seals
nationalgeographic.org/media/crittercam-leopard-seal/
Follow a leopard seal in its natural habitat.

Active Wild: Antarctica Facts
www.activewild.com/antarctica-facts-for-kids/
Check out cool facts and photos of Antarctica.

Index

Published in 2020 by Enslow Publishing, LLC.
101 W. 23rd Street, Suite 240, New York, NY 10011

Library of Congress Cataloging-in-Publication Data

Names: Santos, Rita, author.
Title: Leopard seals / Rita Santos.
Description: New York : Enslow Publishing, 2020 | Series: Life at the poles | Audience: K to grade 4. | Includes bibliographical references and index.
Identifiers: LCCN 2019011909| ISBN 9781978512153 (library bound) | ISBN 9781978512139 (pbk.) | ISBN 9781978512146 (6 pack)
Subjects: LCSH: Leopard seal--Life cycles--Juvenile literature. | Leopard seal--Juvenile literature. | Seals (Animals)--Juvenile literature. | Antarctica--Environmental conditions--Juvenile literature.
Classification: LCC QL737.P64 S357 2020 | DDC 599.79/6--dc23

LC record available at https://lccn.loc.gov/2019011909

Printed in the United States of America

Photos Credits: Leopard Seals – Research by Bruce Donnola

Cover, p. 1 Alexey Seafarer/Shutterstock.com; p. 5 John Dickens/500Px Plus/Getty Images; p. 7 © iStockphoto.com/neosummer; p. 9 Tim Laman/National Geographic Image Collection Magazines/Getty Images; p. 10 Yvonne Pijnenburg-Schonewille/Shutterstock.com; p. 12 Paul Souders/Corbis Documentary/Getty Images; p. 15 Rick Price/Oxford Scientific/Getty Images; p. 17 Paul Nicklen/National Geographic Image Collection/Getty Images; p. 19 NaniP/Shutterstock.com; p. 20 Johner Images/Getty Images; p. 22 Emre Terim/Shutterstock.com; cover and interior pages (frost pattern) polygraphus/Shutterstock.com